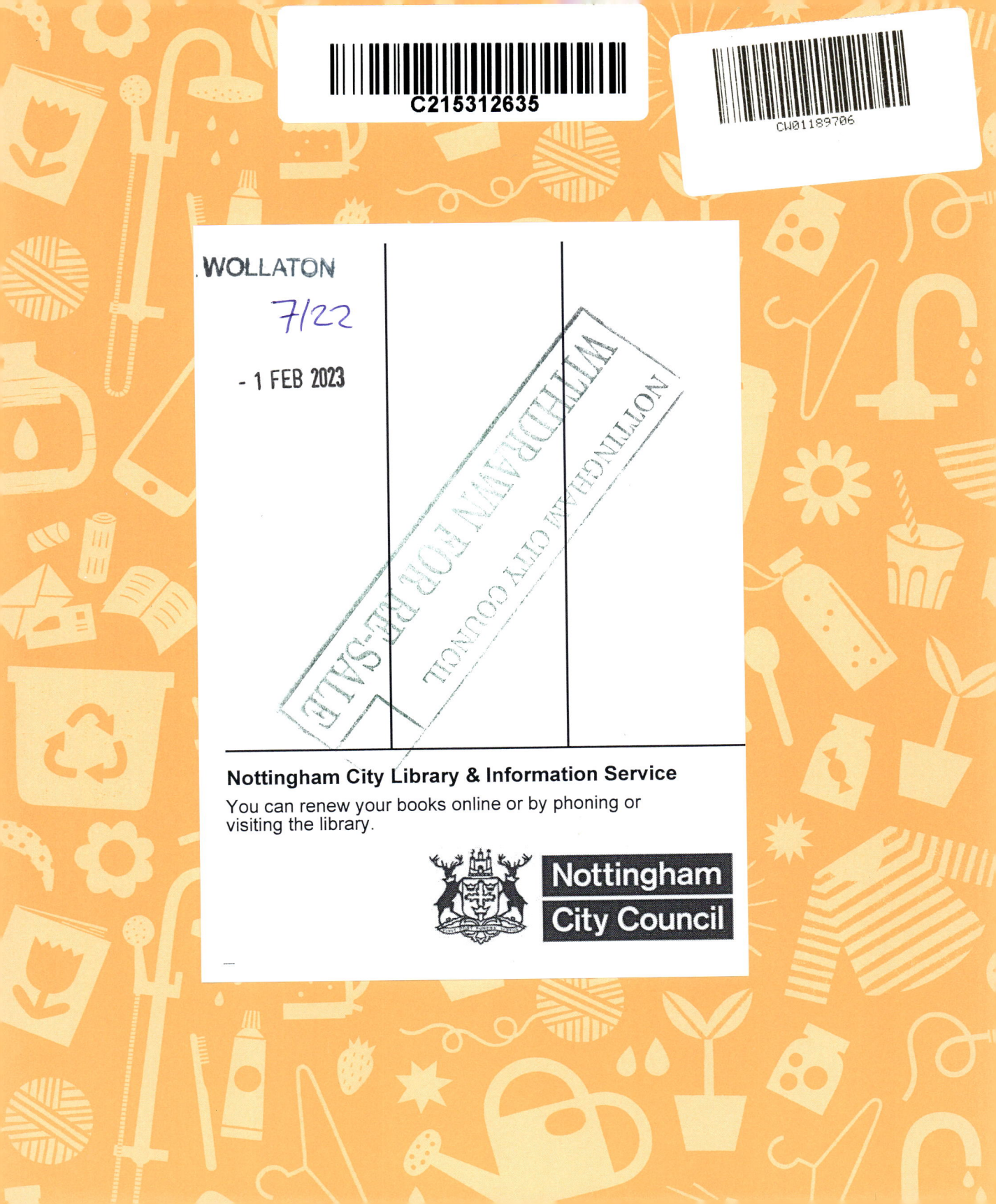

Franklin Watts
First published in Great Britain in 2022 by The Watts Publishing Group

Copyright © The Watts Publishing Group, 2022

All rights reserved.

Credits
Design and project management: Raspberry Books
Art Direction & cover design: Sidonie Beresford-Browne
Designer: Vanessa Mee
Illustrations: Lisa Koesterke

Every attempt has been made to clear copyright. Should there be any inadvertent omission please apply to the publisher for rectification.

HB ISBN: 978 1 4451 8172 1
PB ISBN: 978 1 4451 8173 8

Printed in China

Franklin Watts
An imprint of
Hachette Children's Group
Part of The Watts Publishing Group
Carmelite House
50 Victoria Embankment
London EC4Y 0DZ

An Hachette UK Company
www.hachette.co.uk

www.hachettechildrens.co.uk

BE AN ECO HERO!

AT HOME

Florence Urquhart and Lisa Koesterke

W
FRANKLIN WATTS
LONDON • SYDNEY

CONTENTS

At home 6

Using energy 8

Why save energy? 10

Saving energy 12

Using water 14

Why save water? 16

Saving water 18

Why reduce, reuse, recycle? 20

Reducing waste 22

Reuse and recycle 24

Eco hero activities 26

Quiz 28

Glossary 30

Learn more 31

Index 32

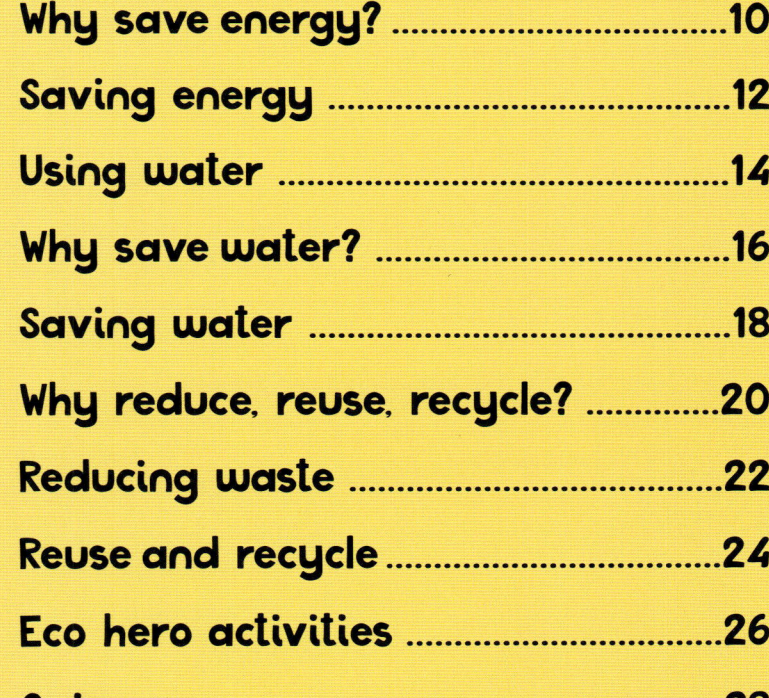

Our homes are full of things that use energy. We use gas for cooking and for heating our homes. We use electricity for lights and to make machines work.

Think of all the things we have in our homes, from furniture to packaging, TVs to clothes. All these things are made using energy.

We use water in lots of ways around the home too. We use it for baths, showers, toilets and cleaning cars.

Energy and water are very important to us. Eco heroes don't waste them!

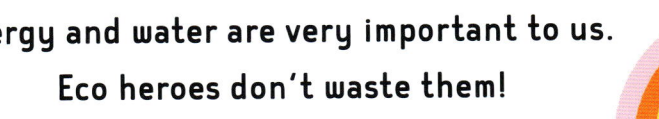

USING ENERGY

We all use a lot of energy such as electricity in our homes every day. Think of all the things we do that use electricity.

All around you there are many other homes using energy too. So if we all save energy, it can make a big difference.

WHY SAVE ENERGY?

Most energy is generated by burning fossil fuels, such as coal. Electricity is generated in power stations and travels along power lines like these to our homes.

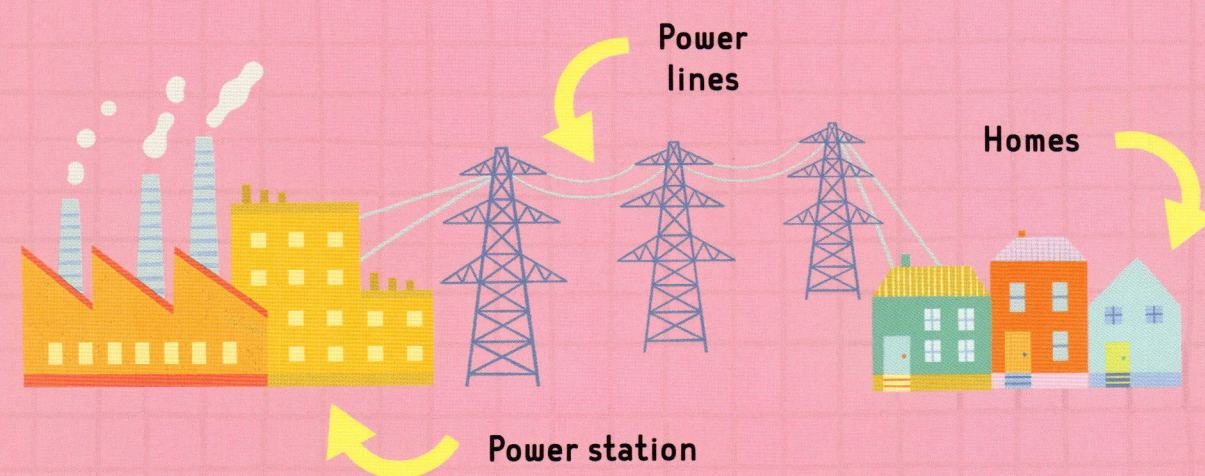

Power lines

Homes

Power station

Fossil fuels will not last forever and we are using them up quickly. Burning fossil fuels also fills the air with dangerous gases.

You can be an eco hero by using less energy. For example, you can help to choose light bulbs that are energy efficient. This means they use less energy and last much longer.

SAVING ENERGY

There are lots of easy ways to save energy.
BE AN ECO HERO BY:

Wearing warm clothes and turning down heating to save energy.

Not leaving TVs, CD players and other items on standby.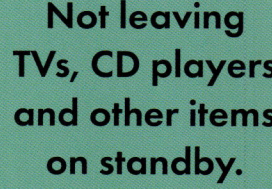

Switching off lights in empty rooms.

Switching off and unplugging mobile phone chargers when not in use.

Reading a book or playing a game instead of watching TV.

USING WATER

We all use a lot of water in our homes every day. Think about all the things you do every day that use water.

Cleaning teeth

Drinking water

Washing hands

Washing clothes

Watering the garden

Flushing the toilet

Can you think of ways to use less water?

15

Water falls from the sky as rain.
It is stored in lakes and reservoirs.
It is cleaned and pumped along pipes
to taps in our homes. This takes energy.

Rainwater

Tap

Clean, fresh water is precious. But, the number of people who live on the planet is growing. We all have to share the supply of water. When there is not enough rain some places can get droughts.

• • • • • • • • • • • • • •

If we all save water, it can make a
big difference. You can be an eco hero
by saving water at home.

SAVING WATER

BE AN ECO HERO BY:

Using a bucket to wash the car, not a hose.

Having a short shower instead of a bath.

Using a watering can, not a hose, to water plants.

Asking an adult to mend dripping taps. A dripping tap wastes four litres of water every day.

Filling the dishwasher: one full load uses less water than several small ones.

Not leaving the tap running while you brush your teeth.

Everything we buy and use is made using energy. Glass, plastic, paper, food, toys, clothes, books and machines are all made using energy and raw materials.

REDUCING WASTE, REUSING AND RECYCLING MEANS:

- less pollution
- less energy and raw materials are used
- less rubbish going to landfill sites

Factories use energy and make pollution.

Our landfill sites are almost full.

REDUCING WASTE

Reducing waste means shopping carefully so you have less rubbish to throw away at home.
BE AN ECO HERO BY:

CHOOSING THINGS WITH LESS PACKAGING.

Buy loose fruit and vegetables.

CHOOSING TO USE REFILLABLE DRINKS BOTTLES.

Choosing packaging such as glass or paper that can be recycled easily.

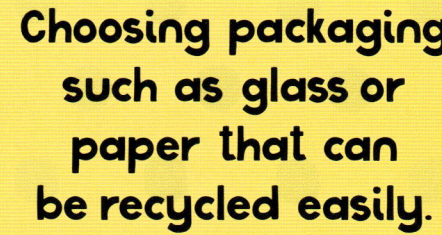

TAKING YOUR OWN BAGS TO THE SHOPS.

Not choosing packaging that is a mix of paper and plastic. It is expensive to recycle.

REUSE AND RECYCLE

You can also save energy by reusing things and recycling. Reusing something makes the most of the time, energy, materials and money used to make it.

Reusing and recycling cuts down pollution and often saves water too.

BE AN ECO HERO AND REUSE THINGS:

Repair and repaint before you replace.

Give old toys and clothes to charity shops.

Choose reusables not disposables.

Be an eco hero by recycling. All these things can be recycled.

SOME PLASTICS

METAL CANS AND TINS

FOOD WASTE

GLASS BOTTLES AND JARS

CLOTHES AND FABRICS

PAPER AND CARD

ECO HERO ACTIVITIES

Here are some ideas that will make your home fit for an eco hero:

STOP THE DRAUGHTS!

Reuse some old socks to make a draught excluder like this. Ask an adult to help.

Stuff old socks with shredded newspaper.

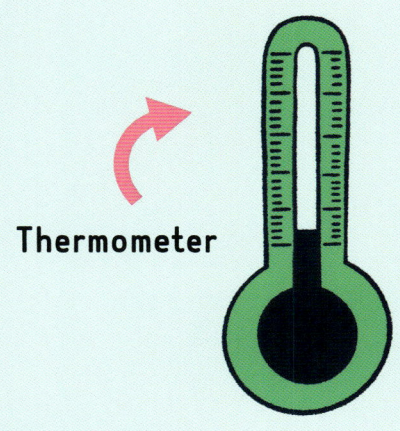

Thermometer

How do the temperatures differ in your house? Which rooms and walls are cooler and which warmer? Use a thermometer to find out. You could put draught excluders in the coldest rooms.

Get crafty!

Think of ways to reuse things. You could turn cereal boxes into magazine racks by covering them in used wrapping paper.

27

QUIZ

1. **Which of these does not use electricity?**
   a. Watching TV
   b. Ironing clothes
   c. Reading a book

2. **What are fossil fuels?**
   a. Materials formed over millions of years from dead animals and plants
   b. Small rocks and stones
   c. Materials made by dinosaurs

3. **What does energy efficient mean?**
   a. When an item uses lots of energy
   b. When an item uses less energy
   c. When an item looks beautiful

4. **Which of these would not be a good way to save energy?**
   a. Switching off lights in empty rooms
   b. Unplugging mobile phone chargers when not in use
   c. Keeping the TV on all night

5. **What is a reservoir?**
   a. A small, dry piece of land
   b. A large lake used to store water
   c. A type of tree

6. **Which of these would not be a good way to save water?**
   a. Mend dripping taps
   b. Leave the tap running while you clean your teeth
   c. Wash the car using a bucket of water

7. What is a landfill site?
a. A small building for storing food
b. A huge hole in the ground where rubbish is buried
c. A large vehicle for driving up steep hills

8. Which of these is a good way to reduce waste?
a. Putting rubbish in the bin
b. Buying more plastic
c. Only using things once

9. What is recycling?
a. Going for a long bicycle ride
b. Putting used toys in the bin
c. Using materials again or making them into something new

10. What will you do to be an eco hero today?

What did you score?

1–3: It would be a good idea to read the book again.

4–6: You're almost there.

7–10: You are an eco hero!

ANSWERS:
1) c. Reading a book
2) a. Materials formed over millions of years from dead animals and plants
3) b. When an item uses less energy
4) c. Keeping the TV on all night
5) b. A large lake used to store water
6) c. Leave the tap running while you clean your teeth
7) b. A huge hole in the ground where rubbish is buried
8) a. Reusing and recycling
9) c. Using materials again or making them into something new

29

GLOSSARY

disposable	an item that is made to be thrown away after it is used.
drought	a long period of time when there is very little rain.
efficient	something that works quickly and well and uses little energy.
electricity	form of energy that makes heat or light that can also be used to make machines work.
energy	something that makes things work, move or change.
fossil fuel	materials found deep under the ground and formed over millions of years from dead animals and plants.
fuel	material used to make heat or light, usually by being burned. Coal, gas and oil are types of fuel.
gas	air-like substance that you cannot see.
generate	to produce energy in a certain form.
landfill site	a huge hole in the ground where rubbish is buried.
litre	a unit for measuring a liquid or gas.
packaging	bottles, packets and boxes used to keep food and other products safe and fresh.
pollution	substance that dirties or poisons air, earth or water.
power station	a factory that generates electricity.
precious	something that has great value because it is rare, expensive or important.
raw material	substance such as wood or oil that is used to make things.
recycling	using materials again or make them into something new.
reservoir	a large lake used to store water.
reusing	using something again.

LEARN MORE

This book shows you some of the ways you can be an eco hero. But there is plenty more you can do to save the planet. Here are some websites that have lots of ideas and information to help you learn more about being an eco hero:

www.recyclenow.com
Website with recycling news and tips for reducing your waste.

www.kidsagainstplastic.co.uk
A UK charity set up by two children to take action against plastic pollution.

For parents and teachers

https://ecofriendlykids.co.uk
This site has information, tips, quizzes and fun games for children, but is ideal for parents who want to share in their kids' adventures as they start to explore ecological issues.

www.wwf.org.uk/get-involved/schools/resources
This site has free curriculum linked resources for teachers to help children explore various environmental issues.

Note to parents and teachers: Every effort has been made by the Publishers to ensure that these websites are suitable for children, that they are of the highest educational value, and that they contain no inappropriate or offensive material. However, because of the nature of the Internet, it is impossible to guarantee that the contents of these sites will not be altered. We strongly advise that Internet access is supervised by a responsible adult.

INDEX

disposables 24, 30
droughts 17, 30

electricity 7, 8, 11, 12, 28, 30
energy 7, 8, 9, 11, 12, 17, 21, 24, 28, 30

food 21, 25
fossil fuels 11, 28, 30

glass 21, 23, 25

heating 7, 12

landfill sites 21, 29, 30

metal 25

packaging 7, 22, 23, 30
paper 21, 23, 25, 26, 27
plastics 21, 23, 25

pollution 21, 24, 30
power stations 11, 30

raw materials 21, 24, 30
recycle 20, 21, 23, 24, 25, 26, 29, 30, 31
reducing waste 20, 21, 22, 23, 29
reuse 20, 21, 24, 26, 27, 30
rubbish 21, 22

saving energy 9, 10, 11, 12, 13, 24, 28
saving water 14, 16, 17, 18, 19, 24, 28

water 7, 14, 15, 16, 17, 24, 28, 31